Mel Bay Presents

50 Three-Chord Christmas Songs

for Guitar, Banjo, and Uke

by Larry McCabe

1 2 3 4 5 6 7 8 9 0

© 2009 BY MEL BAY PUBLICATIONS, INC., PACIFIC, MO 63069.
ALL RIGHTS RESERVED. INTERNATIONAL COPYRIGHT SECURED. B.M.I. MADE AND PRINTED IN U.S.A.
No part of this publication may be reproduced in whole or in part, or stored in a retrieval system, or transmitted in any form
or by any means, electronic, mechanical, photocopy, recording, or otherwise, without written permission of the publisher.

Visit us on the Web at www.melbay.com — E-mail us at email@melbay.com

CONTENTS

CHORDS USED IN THIS BOOK 3
EASY CHORD STRUMS 4
5-STRING BANJO ROLLS 5
SINGING THE SONGS 6
A Babe is Born All of a May 8
A Little Child on Earth Has Been Born 9
All Through the Night 10
Angels We Have Heard on High 11
As With Gladness Men of Old 12
Auld Lang Syne 15
Away in a Manger 16
The Boar's Head Carol 18
Born is He, This Holy Child 19
The Cherry Tree Carol 21
Child in the Manger 22
Christmas is Coming 24
The Christmas Tree with its Candles Bright 25
Christ Was Born in Bethlehem 26
Christ Was Born on Christmas Day 27
Come, Thou Almighty King 29
Ding Dong Merrily on High 30
The First Noel 32
The Friendly Beasts 34
Glad Christmas Bells 35
God Bless the Master of This House 36
Good Christian Men, Rejoice 39
Good King Wenceslas 40
Go Tell It on the Mountain 42
Hark! the Herald Angels Sing 44
Here We Come A-Caroling 45
The Holly and the Ivy 46
The Holly Bears a Berry (The St. Day Carol) 48
Infant Holy, Infant Lowly 49
In the Silence of the Night 50
I Saw Three Ships 51
Jingle Bells 52
Joy to the World 54
Let Our Gladness Know No End 55
Let Us Go, O Shepherds 56
Love Came Down at Christmas 57
Mary Had a Baby 58
O Come, Little Children 59
Oh Christmas Tree 60
Once in Royal David's City 62
Out of the Orient Crystal Skies 64
Over the River and Through the Woods 65
The Seven Blessings of Mary 66
Shepherds, Shake off Your Drowsy Sleep 68
Silent Night 70
Sussex Carol (On Christmas Night, All Christians Sing) 71
Up on the Housetop 72
The Virgin Mary Had a Baby Boy 74
We Wish You a Merry Christmas 76
While Shepherds Watched Their Flocks by Night 78

CHORDS USED IN THIS BOOK

X Do not play this string   **1** First finger (index)   **3** Third finger (ring)

O Play this string open   **2** Second finger (middle)   **4** Fourth finger (little)

You can accompany every song in every song in this book using only three chords: G, C, and D7!

GUITAR CHORDS

Beginning guitar players can start with the chords shown at the right:

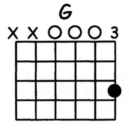 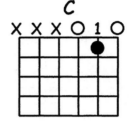 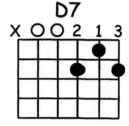

You can also play the "complete" C and G chords shown at the right. Notice that there are two possible fingerings for the six-string G.

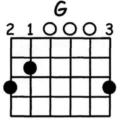 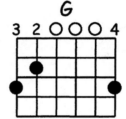 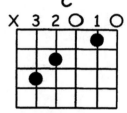

5-STRING BANJO CHORDS

The open fifth string (not shown) can be strummed with both G and C. It sounds better if the fifth string is omitted when strumming D7.

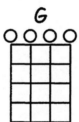 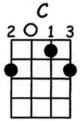 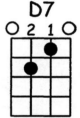

UKULELE CHORDS

Tune the uke G-C-E-A. Tip: The first finger (index) holds down (barres) three strings when playing D7.

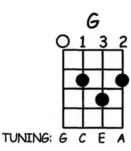 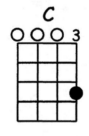 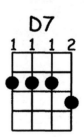

THE D CHORD

Pro tip: It is often possible to use a D chord (right) in place of D7. You can do this any time you feel that the sound of the music is improved by the substitution.

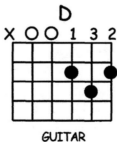 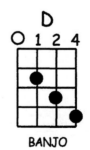 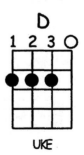

GUITAR   BANJO   UKE

EASY CHORD STRUMS

• You can strum chords with either a pick or your thumb.
• Play any chord(s) you like to practice these easy strums.

4/4 means "four beats to the measure." The easiest way to play in 4/4 is to strum four times in each measure. Use a down-pick motion ⊓ and count "one two three four," strumming a chord on each count:

Strum twice in each measure for songs in 2/4 time: Strum three times per measure for songs in 3/4 time:

The simple 2/4 strum above can also be used in *cut time* ¢ (cut time also has two beats per measure).

The plain *downbeat* strum can be livened up by adding *upbeat* strums. Pick the upbeat strums with an upward motion of the pick ∨ (or thumb, if you are strumming with your thumb). The following example, in 4/4 time, is counted "one and two and three and four and":

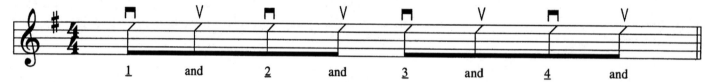

For variety, combine quarter-note strums with eighth-note strums. The next two examples show possibilities in 3/4 time:

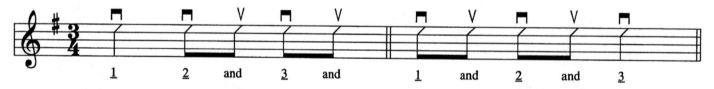

Here are two typical "combination strums" in 4/4 time:

> **TIP:** To apply a *4/4* pattern to *cut time*, tap your foot two times (instead of four times) per measure.

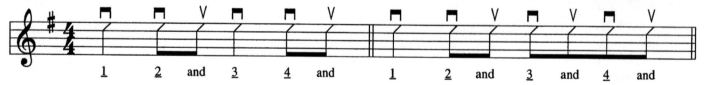

And two basic strums for 6/8 time:

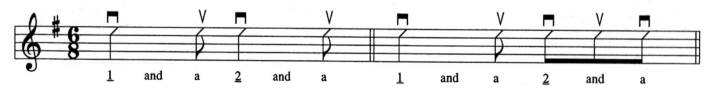

© 2009 by Mel Bay Publications, Inc. (BMI.). All rights Reserved.

5-STRING BANJO ROLLS

4/4 rolls can also be applied to *cut time*. For cut time, tap your foot two times per measure instead of four times.

© 2009 by Mel Bay Publications, Inc. (BMI.). All rights Reserved.

SINGING THE SONGS

THE STARTING NOTE

A "starting note" is given at the beginning of each song. <u>The starting note is the pitch of the first note of the song as it relates to the guitar.</u> For example, if the starting note is the "open fourth string," you can pluck that guitar string to hear the first note of the song.

A five-string banjo can also be used to find the starting note for songs that start on strings 2, 3, and 4. Our "starting note" concept cannot be applied to ukuleles.

CHANGING THE OCTAVE OR THE KEY

All the songs in this book are in the key of G major. Singers will sometimes find it helpful to sing a song one octave lower or higher than it is written. After deciding on the octave for the starting note, sing through several bars of the song to see if the melody "fits" your voice.

All singers will find that, for some songs, the key of G is not their best vocal key. If a song is difficult to sing in G, the guitarist can use a *capo* (a simple clamp, available at any music store) to *transpose* from G to a more suitable vocal key. The capo is placed at the appropriate fret (see below), and the picker can still strum the G, C, and D7 chords without having to learn new chord fingerings in new keys.

It is sometimes desirable to change keys for the purpose of accomodating an instrumentalist.

Ukulele players can use a capo, too (use a mandolin capo if you can't find a uke capo). Banjo players can use a capo, but the fifth string must also be capoed with a special *fifth-string capo.*

USING THE CAPO TO CHANGE KEYS

Each fret represents a half-step increase in pitch. Therefore, if the capo is placed at the first fret, and the chords are played in G, the actual key will be A-flat (A-flat is one-half step higher than G).

The following list shows the "actual" key when the capo is used while playing chords in the key of G:

First fret = Key of <u>A flat</u>

Second fret = Key of <u>A</u>

Third fret = Key of <u>B flat</u>

Fourth fret = Key of <u>B</u>

Fifth fret = Key of <u>C</u>

<u>In practice, the capo is seldom used beyond the fifth fret.</u> Nevertheless, here are some higher capo positions as they relate to the key of G:

Sixth fret = Key of <u>D flat</u>

Seventh fret = Key of <u>D</u>

Eighth fret = Key of <u>E flat</u>

Ninth fret = Key of <u>E</u>

Tenth fret = Key of <u>F</u>

Of course, another way to change keys is to transpose the melody and chords to the new key, and play the chords in the new key instead of using the capo. The subject of transposing without using a capo is beyond the scope of this book; see a music teacher if you are not sure how to do this.

A Babe Is Born All of a May

Starting note: Open third string.

Words, 15th Century England
French Melody

A Babe is born all of____ a may,* To

bring sal - va - tion un - to us; To

Him we sing both night____ and day: Ve -

ni cre - a____ - tor Spi - re - tus.**

* maiden
** O come, Creator Spirit

At Bethlehem, that blessed place,
The child of bliss now born he was;
And him to serve God give us grace,
O lux beata Trinitas.
(O Trinity blessed light)

There came three kings out of the East,
To worship the King that is so free,
With gold and myrrh and frankincense,
A solis ortus cardine.
(Risen from the quarter of the sun)

The angels came down with one cry,
A fair song that night sung they
In worship of that child:
Gloria tibi Domine.
(Glory to Thee, O Lord)

A babe is born all of a may,
To bring salvation unto us.
To him we sing both night and day.
Veni Creator Spiritus. Noell
(O Come, Creator Spirit)

Arr. © 2009 by Mel Bay Publications, Inc. (BMI.). All rights Reserved.

A Little Child on the Earth Has Been Born

Starting note: Open third string.

Flemish Carol

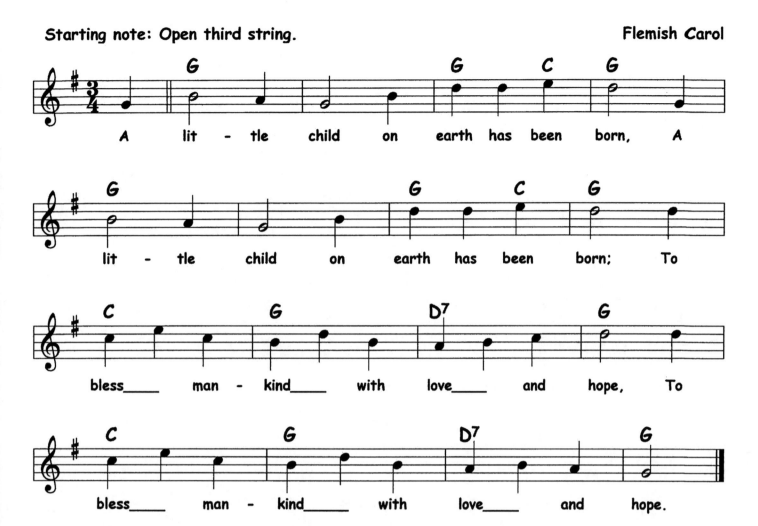

Within no palace did He dwell,
Within no palace did he dwell;
He is the King from Israel,
He is the King from Israel.

He bore the cross, His love was strong,
He bore the cross, His love was strong;
He taught the people right from wrong,
He taught the people right from wrong.

Arr. © 2009 by Mel Bay Publications, Inc. (BMI.). All rights Reserved.

All Through the Night

Starting note: Open third string.

Traditional Welsh Carol

Sleep, my child and peace at-tend Thee, All through the night:

Guard - ian an - gels God will send Thee, All through the night.

Soft the drow - sy hours are creep-ing, Hill and vale in slum - ber sleep-ing;

God, His lov - ing vig - il keep-ing, All through the night.

While the moon her watch is keeping,
All through the night;
While the weary world is sleeping,
All through the night.
Through your dreams you're swiftly stealing,
Visions of delight revealing;
Christmas time is so appealing,
All through the night.

You, my God, a Babe of wonder,
All through the night;
Dreams you dream can't break from thunder,
All through the night.
Children's dreams can not be broken,
Life is but a lovely token;
Christmas should be soft and spoken,
All through the night.

Arr. © 2009 by Mel Bay Publications, Inc. (BMI.). All rights Reserved.

Angels We Have Heard on High

Starting note: Open second string.

Traditional French Carol
Translated by James Chadwick (1813-1882)

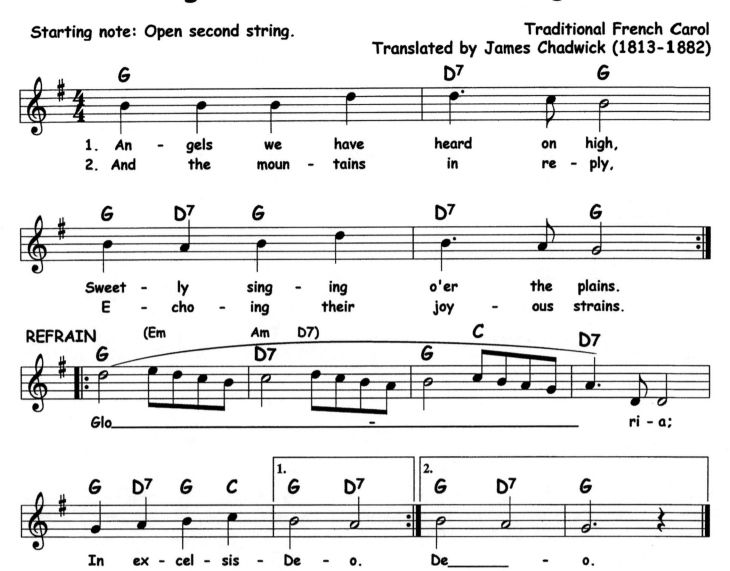

( ) Chords enclosed in parenthesis are optional.

2. Shepherds, why this jubilee?
   Why your joyous strains prolong?
   What the gladsome tidings be
   Which inspire your heavenly song?
   Refrain

3. Come to Bethlehem and see
   Him whose birth the angels sing;
   Come, adore on bended knee,
   Christ the Lord, the newborn King.
   Refrain

4. See Him in a manger laid,
   Whom the choirs of angels praise;
   Mary, Joseph, lend your aid,
   While our hearts in love we raise.
   Refrain

Arr. © 2009 by Mel Bay Publications, Inc. (BMI.). All rights Reserved.

As with Gladness Men of Old

Starting note: Open third string.

Words by William C. Dix (1837-1898)
Music by Konrad Kocher (1786-1872)

Arr. © 2009 by Mel Bay Publications, Inc. (BMI.). All rights Reserved.

As they offered gifts most rare
At that manger rude and bare,
So may we with holy joy,
Pure and free from sin's alloy;
All our costliest treasures bring,
Christ, to Thee, our heavenly King.

Holy Jesus, every day
Keep us in the narrow way,
And, when earthly things are past,
Bring our ransomed souls at last;
Where they need no star to guide,
Where no clouds Thy glory hide.

In the heavenly country bright,
Need they no created light,
Thou its Light, its Joy, its Crown,
Thou its Sun which goes not down;
There forever may we sing
Alleluias to our King!

Auld Lang Syne

Starting note: Open fourth string.

Words by Robert Burns
Scottish Air

Arr. © 2009 by Mel Bay Publications, Inc. (BMI.). All rights Reserved.

Away in a Manger

Starting note: Second string, third fret.

American Carol

Arr. © 2009 by Mel Bay Publications, Inc. (BMI.). All rights Reserved.

The cattle are lowing, the poor baby wakes,
But little Lord Jesus no crying He makes;
I love Thee, Lord Jesus, look down from the sky,
And stay by my cradle to watch lullaby.

Be near me, Lord Jesus,
I ask Thee to stay
Close by me forever and love me, I pray;
Bless all the dear children in Thy tender care,
And take us to heaven to live with Thee there.

The Boar's Head Carol

Starting note: Open fourth string.

Traditional English Carol

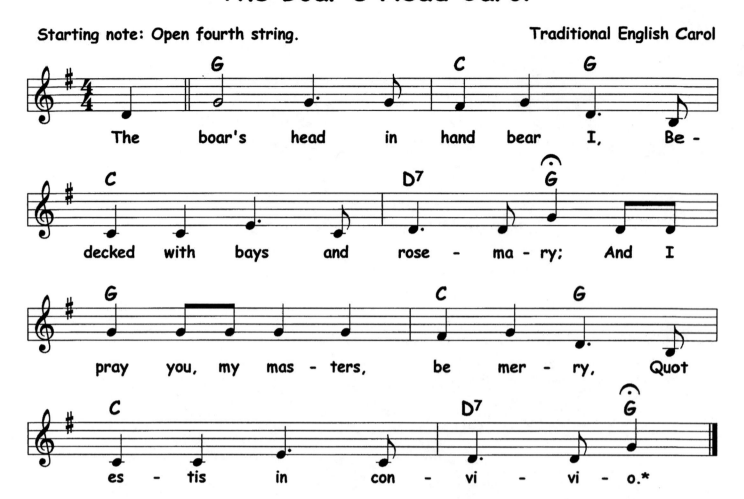

The boar's head in hand bear I, Be -
decked with bays and rose - ma - ry; And I
pray you, my mas - ters, be mer - ry, Quot
es - tis in con - vi - vi - o.*

* Quot estis in convivio. Translation: You who are at this feast.

Evidently this traditional English carol dates back to perhaps as early as the 16th century. It is interesting to note that, even though few of us partake in boar's head these days, the spices mentioned in the first verse are still in common use.

This song does have a chorus, and it is even stranger than the verses, and often omitted from performances today. I too have omitted the chorus here, to spare us all the agony of trying to decipher the pronunciation of its odd words.

The boar's head, as I understand,
Is the rarest dish in all this land;
Which thus bedecked with a gay garland
Let us servire cantico. (Let us serve with a song)

Our steward hath provided this
In honor of the King of Bliss;
Which, on this day to be served is
In Reginensi atrio. (In the Queen's hall)

Arr. © 2009 by Mel Bay Publications, Inc. (BMI.). All rights Reserved.

Born is He, This Holy Child

Starting note: Open fourth string.

Traditional French Carol

See Him lying peacefully
On His tiny bed of hay;
See Him lying in stable bare,
O what gracious a Lord is there!
Chorus

Jesus! Thou all-powerful Lord,
Now as Baby art Thou adored;
Jesus! Thou all-powerful King,
All our hearts to Thee we bring.
Chorus

Arr. © 2009 by Mel Bay Publications, Inc. (BMI.). All rights Reserved.

The Cherry Tree Carol

Starting note: Open third string.

Traditional English Carol

As Jo - seph was a walk___ - ing, He
heard an an - gel sing, "This
night shall be the birth___ - time of___
Christ, the___ heav'n - ly King."

He neither shall be born
In housen nor in hall;
Nor in the place of paradise,
But in an ox's stall.

He neither shall be clothed
In purple nor in pall;
But in the fair white linen
That usen babies all.

He neither shall be rocked
In silver nor in gold;
But in a wooden manger
That resteth on the mould.

Arr. © 2009 by Mel Bay Publications, Inc. (BMI.). All rights Reserved.

Child in the Manger

Starting note: Sixth string, third fret.

Words by Lachlan MacBean (1853-1931)
Traditional Gaelic Melody

This traditional Gaelic melody is the basis of several songs, including the well-known "Morning Has Broken." The lyrics used here are from Lachlan MacBean's 1888 songbook entitled *Songs and Hymns of the Scottish Highlands.*

Arr. © 2009 by Mel Bay Publications, Inc. (BMI.). All rights Reserved.

Monarchs have tender, delicate children,
Nourished in splendor, proud and gay;
Death soon shall banish honor and beauty,
Pleasure shall vanish, forms decay.

But the most holy Child of salvation,
Gentle and lowly lived below;
Now as our glorious mighty Redeemer,
See Him victorious o'er each foe.

Prophets foretold Him - infant of wonder,
Angels behold him on His throne;
Worthy our Savior of all their praises,
Happy forever are His own.

Christmas is Coming

Starting note: First string, third fret.

Traditional

Christ - mas   is   com - ing,   The   goose   is   get - ting   fat,

Please   to   put   a   pen - ny   in   the   old   man's___   hat;

Please   to   put   a   pen - ny   in   the   old   man's___   hat.

If you have no penny,
A half-penny will do,
If you have no half-penny,
Then God bless you!
If you have no half-penny,
Then God bless you!

Christmas is coming,
Lights are on the tree,
Hang up your stocking
For Santa Claus to see;
Hang up your stocking
For Santa Claus to see.

If you you have no stocking,
A little sock will do;
If you have no little sock,
Then God bless you!
If you have no little sock,
Then God bless you!

Christmas is coming,
The season of good cheer,
Let's all sing a carol
For the brand-new year!
Let's all sing a carol
For the brand-new year!

If you have no carol,
A jolly song will do;
If you have no jolly songs,
God bless you!
If you have no jolly songs,
God bless you!

Arr. © 2009 by Mel Bay Publications, Inc. (BMI.). All rights Reserved.

The Christmas Tree with Its Candles Bright

Starting note: Open third string.

Traditional German Carol

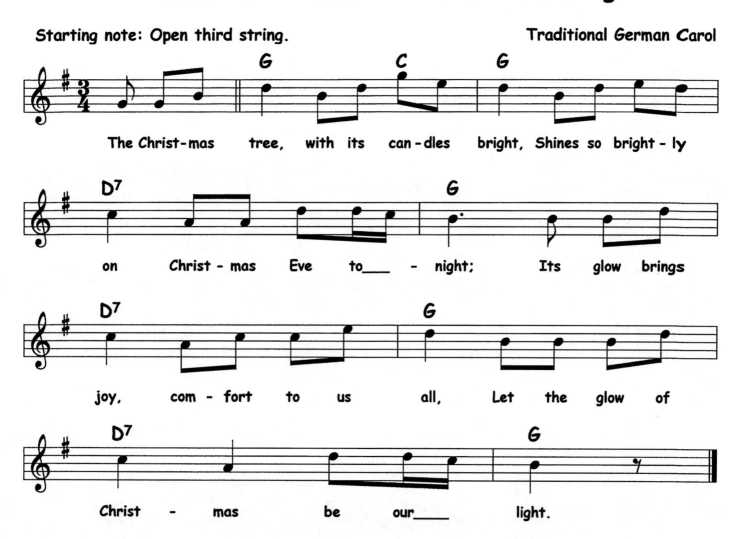

The Christ-mas tree, with its can-dles bright, Shines so bright - ly
on Christ - mas Eve to___ - night; Its glow brings
joy, com - fort to us all, Let the glow of
Christ - mas be our____ light.

The children stand round the gleaming tree,
Sparkling eyes enchanted by candles so bright;
The shining symbol of Christmas season
Reminds us always follow the light.

Arr. © 2009 by Mel Bay Publications, Inc. (BMI.). All rights Reserved.

Christ Was Born in Bethlehem

Starting note: Open second string.

American, Mid-20th Cent.

Arr. © 2009 by Mel Bay Publications, Inc. (BMI.). All rights Reserved.

Christ Was Born on Christmas Day

Starting note: Second string, third fret.

From *Piae Cantiones* (1582)

Christ was born on Christ - mas Day,

Wreath the hol - ly, twine the bay,

Light and life and joy is He, The

Babe, the Son, the Ho - ly One of Mar - y.

He is born to set us free,
He is born our Lord to be;
Carol, Christians, joyfully
The God, the Lord, by all ador'd forever.

Let the bright red berries glow,
Ev'ry where in goodly show;
Light and life and joy is He
The Babe, the Son, the Holy One of Mary.

Christian men, rejoice and sing,
'Tis the birthday of a King;
Carol, Christians, joyfully
The God, the Lord, by all ador'd forever.

Arr. © 2009 by Mel Bay Publications, Inc. (BMI.). All rights Reserved.

Come, Thou Almighty King

Starting note: Second string, third fret.

Author of Lyrics Unknown (1757)
Music by Felice Giardini, 1769

Come, Thou Al - might____ - y King, Help us Thy
name____ to sing, Help us to praise;
Fa - ther! all glo - ri - ous, O'er all vic - to - ri - ous,
Come and reign o - ver us, An - cient of days.

Come, Thou incarnate Word,
Gird on Thy mighty sword,
Our pray'r attend;
Come, and Thy people bless,
And give Thy word success,
Spirit of holiness!
On us descend.

Come, holy Comforter!
Thy sacred witness bear,
In this glad hour;
Thou who almighty art,
Now rule in ev'ry heart,
And ne'er from us depart,
Spirit of pow'r!

Arr. © 2009 by Mel Bay Publications, Inc. (BMI.). All rights Reserved.

Ding Dong! Merrily on High

Starting note: Open third string.

Traditional French Carol

Arr. © 2009 by Mel Bay Publications, Inc. (BMI.). All rights Reserved.

Ding dong merrily on high,
In heav'n the bells are ringing;
Ding dong! verily the sky
Is riv'n with angel singing.
Refrain

E'en so here below, below,
Let steeple bells be swungen;
And "Io, io, io!"
By priest and people sungen.
Refrain

Pray you, dutifully prime
Your matin' chime, ye ringers;
May you beautifully rime
Your evetime song, ye singers.
Refrain

The First Noel

Starting note: Open second string

Traditional English Carol

Arr. © 2009 by Mel Bay Publications, Inc. (BMI.). All rights Reserved.

They looked up and saw a star
Shining in the East, beyond them far:
And to the earth it gave great light,
And so it continued both day and night.

Refrain

And by the light of that same star,
Three wise men came from country far;
To seek for a King was their intent,
And to follow the star wherever it went.

Refrain

This star drew nigh to the northwest,
O'er Bethlehem it took its rest;
And there it did both stop and stay,
Right over the place where Jesus lay.

Refrain

Then entered in those wise men three,
Full reverently upon their knee;
And offered there in His presence,
Their gold, and myrrh, and frankincense.

Refrain

HEUREUX NOËL

The Friendly Beasts

Starting note: Open third string.

Lyrics by Robert Davis (1881-1950)
Music from *Orientus Partibus* (12th cent. Latin)

2. Jesus our brother, kind and good
   Was humbly born in a stable rude
   And the friendly beasts around Him stood,
   Jesus our brother, kind and good.

3. "I," said the donkey, shaggy and brown,
   "I carried His mother up hill and down;
   I carried her safely to Bethlehem town."
   "I," said the donkey, shaggy and brown.

4. "I," said the cow all white and red
   "I gave Him my manger for His bed;
   I gave him my hay to pillow his head."
   "I," said the cow all white and red.

5. "I," said the dove from the rafters high,
   "I cooed Him to sleep so He would not cry;
   We cooed Him to sleep, my mate and I."
   "I," said the dove from the rafters high.

6. Thus every beast by some good spell,
   In the stable dark was glad to tell
   Of the gift he gave Immanuel,
   The gift he gave Immanuel.

7. "I," was glad to tell
   Of the gift they gave Immanuel,
   The gift they gave Immanuel.
   Jesus our brother, kind and good.

Arr. © 2009 by Mel Bay Publications, Inc. (BMI.). All rights Reserved.

Glad Christmas Bells

Starting note: Open fourth string.

Traditional

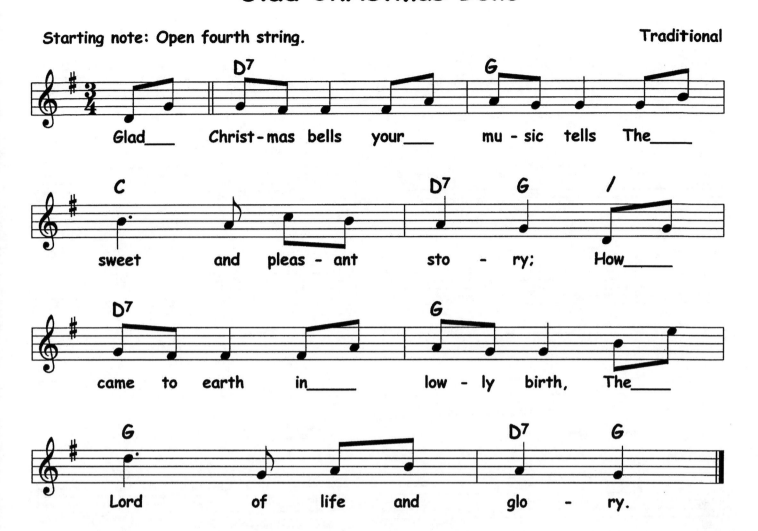

Glad___ Christ-mas bells your___ mu - sic tells The___
sweet and pleas - ant sto - ry; How___
came to earth in___ low - ly birth, The___
Lord of life and glo - ry.

No palace hall its ceiling tall
His kingly head spread over;
There only stood a stable rude,
The heavenly Babe to cover.

No raiment gay, as there He lay,
Adorned the infant Stranger;
Poor, humble Child of mother mild,
She laid Him in a manger.

But from afar, a splendid star,
The wise men westward turning;
The livelong night saw pure and bright,
Above His birthplace burning.

Arr. © 2009 by Mel Bay Publications, Inc. (BMI.). All rights Reserved.

God Bless the Master of This House

Starting note: Open third string.

Traditional Cornish Carol

Arr. © 2009 by Mel Bay Publications, Inc. (BMI.). All rights Reserved.

Then let us all most merry be,
And sing with cheerful voice-a;
For we have good occasion now
This time for to rejoice-a.
Chorus

Then sing with voices cheerfully,
For Christ this time was born-a;
Who did from death deliver us
When we were left forlorn-a.
Chorus

Good Christian Men, Rejoice

Starting note: Open third string.

English Lyrics by John Mason Neale (1818-1866)
14th Century German Carol

Good Chris-tian men, re - joice_____ With heart, and soul, and voice:_____

Give ye heed to what we say: News! News! Je - sus Christ is born to-day!

Ox and ass be - fore Him bow, And He is in the man - ger now;

Christ is born to - day!_____ Christ is born to - day!

Good Christian men, rejoice
With heart, and soul, and voice;
Now ye hear of endless bliss:
Joy! Joy!
Jesus Christ was born for this!
He hath ope'd the heav'nly door,
And man is blessed evermore;
Christ was born for this!
Christ was born for this!

Good Christian men, rejoice
With heart, and soul, and voice;
Now ye need not fear the grave:
Peace! Peace!
Jesus Christ was born to save!
Calls you one and calls you all,
To gain His everlasting hall;
Christ was born to save!
Christ was born to save!

Arr. © 2009 by Mel Bay Publications, Inc. (BMI.). All rights Reserved.

Good King Wenceslas

Starting note: Open third string.

Words by Rev. J.M. Neale, 1853
Scandanavian Melody, 1582

Good King Wen-ces-las looked out On the feast of Ste-phen,

When the snow lay 'round a-bout, Deep and crisp and e-ven.

Bright-ly shone the moon that night, Though the frost was cru-el,

When a poor man came in sight, Gath-'ring win-ter fu_____-el.

Arr. © 2009 by Mel Bay Publications, Inc. (BMI.). All rights Reserved.

"Hither, page, and stand by me,
If thou know'st it, telling,
Yonder peasant, who is he?
Where and what his dwelling?"
"Sire, he lives a good league hence,
Underneath the mountain,
Right against the forest fence,
By Saint Agnes' fountain."

"Bring me flesh and bring me wine
Bring me pine logs hither;
Thou and I will see him dine
When we bear him thither."
Page and monarch, forth they went,
Forth they went together;
Through the rude wind's wild lament,
And the bitter weather.

"Sire, the night is darker now,
And the wind blows stronger;
Fails my heart, I know not how;
I can go no longer."
"Mark my footsteps my good page,
Tread thou in them boldly;
Thou shalt find the winter's rage
Freeze thy blood less coldly."

In his master's steps he trod,
Where the snow lay dinted;
Heat was in the very sod
Which the Saint had printed.
Therefore, Christian men, be sure,
Wealth or rank possessing,
Ye who now will bless the poor,
Shall yourselves find blessing.

Go Tell It on the Mountain

Starting note: Open second string.

Traditional Spiritual

Arr. © 2009 by Mel Bay Publications, Inc. (BMI.). All rights Reserved.

He made me a watchman
Upon the city wall;
And if I am a Christian,
I am the least of all.
Chorus

The shepherds kept their watching,
When lo! Above the earth
Rang out the angel chorus
That hailed our Saviour's birth.
Chorus

Hark! The Herald Angels Sing

Starting note: Open fourth string.

Orig. Lyrics by Charles Wesley, 1739
Music and additional lyrics by many others

Hark! the her - ald an - gels sing,___ "Glo - ry to the new - born King!

Peace on earth and mer - cy mild,___ God and sin - ners rec - on - ciled."

Joy - ful all ye na - tions rise,___ Join the tri - umph of the skies;___

With an - gel - ic host pro - claim, "Christ is__ born in Beth - le - hem."

REFRAIN

Hark! the her - ald an - gels sing, "Glo - ry__ to the new - born King."

Hail the heav'nly Prince of Peace!
Hail the Sun of Righteousness!
Light and life to all He brings,
Ris'n with healing in His wings.
Mild He lays His glory by,
Born that man no more may die;
Born to raise the sons of earth,
Born to give them second birth.
Refrain

Come, Desire of nations, come,
Fix in us Thy humble home;
Rise, the woman's conqu'ring Seed,
Bruise in us the serpent's head.
Now display Thy saving power,
Ruined nature now restore;
Now in mystic union join
Thine to ours, and ours to Thine.
Refrain

Arr. © 2009 by Mel Bay Publications, Inc. (BMI.). All rights Reserved.

Here We Come A-Caroling

Starting note: Open third string.

Traditional English Carol

Here we come a - car - ol - ing A - mong the leaves so green;

Here we come a - wan - d'ring so fair____ to be seen.

REFRAIN

Love and joy come to you, And to you glad tid - ings too; And God

bless you and send___ you a Hap____ - py New Year, And God

send you a Hap____ - py New Year._____

We are not daily beggars
That beg from door to door;
But we are neighbors' children,
Whom you have seen before.
Refrain

Good master and mistress,
As you sit by the fire;
Pray think of us poor children,
Who wander in the mire.
Refrain

Arr. © 2009 by Mel Bay Publications, Inc. (BMI.). All rights Reserved.

The Holly and the Ivy

Starting note: Open third string.

Traditional English

Arr. © 2009 by Mel Bay Publications, Inc. (BMI.). All rights Reserved.

The holly bears a blossom
As white as the lily flower;
And Mary bore sweet Jesus Christ,
To be our sweet Savior.
Refrain

The holly bears a berry
As red as any blood;
And Mary bore sweet Jesus Christ
To do poor sinners good.
Refrain

The holly bears a prickle,
As sharp as any thorn;
And Mary bore sweet Jesus Christ
On Christmas Day in the morn.
Refrain

The holly bears a bark
As bitter as any gall;
And Mary bore sweet Jesus Christ
For to redeem us all.
Refrain

The Holly Bears a Berry
(The St. Day Carol)

Starting note: Open third string.

Traditional English Carol

Now the holly bears a berry as green as the grass;
And Mary bore Jesus, who died on the cross:
Refrain

Now the holly bears a berry as black as the coal;
And Mary bore Jesus, who died for us all.
Refrain

Now the holly bears a berry, as blood is it red;
Then trust we our Saviour, who rose from the dead.
Refrain

Arr. © 2009 by Mel Bay Publications, Inc. (BMI.). All rights Reserved.

Infant Holy, Infant Lowly

Starting note: Open fourth string.

Traditional Polish Carol

Arr. © 2009 by Mel Bay Publications, Inc. (BMI.). All rights Reserved.

In the Silence of the Night

Starting note: Open third string.

Traditional Polish Carol

In the___ si - lence of that night so bright,

Came the___ song of an - gels snow - y white;

Come, o wise men, rise and jour - ney To the stall where Je - sus lies with

Ma - ry by His side.

Arr. © 2009 by Mel Bay Publications, Inc. (BMI.). All rights Reserved.

I Saw Three Ships

Starting note: Open fourth string.

Traditional English Carol

I saw three ships come sail - ing in, On

Christ - mas Day, on Christ - mas Day; I saw three ships come

sail - ing in, On Christ - mas Day in the morn - ing.

And what was in those ships all three,
On Christmas Day, on Christmas Day;
And what was in those ships all three,
On Christmas Day in the morning.

The Virgin Mary and Christ were there,
On Christmas Day, on Christmas Day;
The Virgin Mary and Christ were there,
On Christmas Day in the morning.

Arr. © 2009 by Mel Bay Publications, Inc. (BMI.). All rights Reserved.

Jingle Bells

Starting note: Open second string.

James Pierpont, 1857

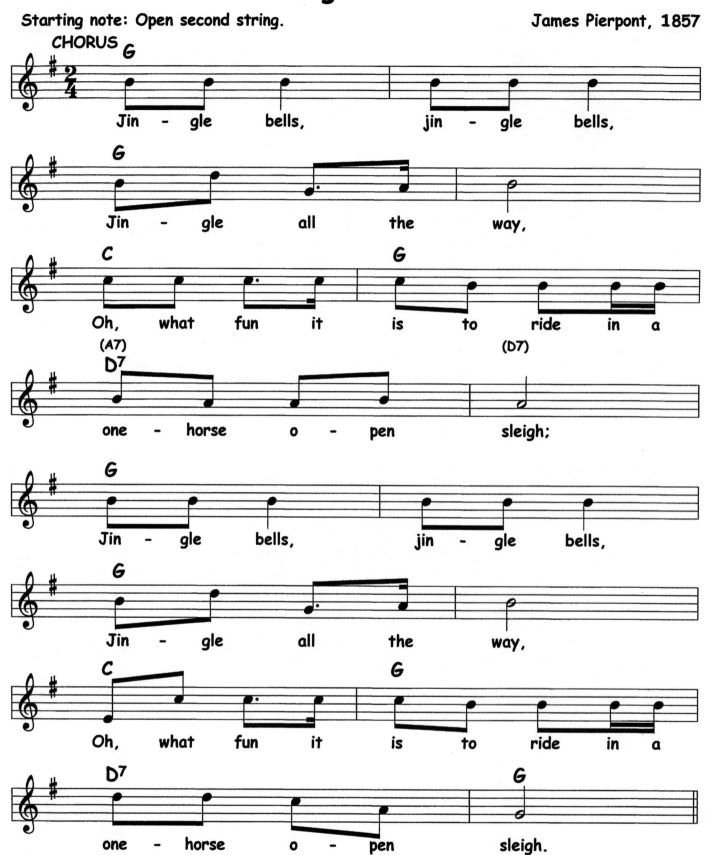

Arr. © 2009 by Mel Bay Publications, Inc. (BMI.). All rights Reserved.

The familiar chorus of this Christmas classic somehow experienced a melodic transformation, and today it is sung and played different than Mr. Pierpont's original tune.

Joy to the World

Starting note: First string, third fret.

Words by Isaac Watts, 1719
Music by Lowell Mason, 1836

Joy to the world! The Lord is come; Let earth re - ceive her King; Let ev__ - 'ry__ heart_____ Pre - pare__ Him__ room_____ And heav'n and na - ture__ sing, And__ heav'n and na - ture__ sing, And___ heav'n___ and heav'n_____ and na - ture sing.

Joy to the world! the Savior reigns;
Let men their songs employ.
While field and floods,
Rocks, hills, and plains
Repeat the sounding joy,
Repeat the sounding joy,
Repeat, repeat the sounding joy.

He rules the world with truth and grace,
And makes the nations prove
The glories of His righteousness,
And wonders of His love,
And wonders of His love,
And wonders, wonders of His love.

Arr. © 2009 by Mel Bay Publications, Inc. (BMI.). All rights Reserved.

Let Our Gladness Know No End

Starting note: Open third string.

Traditional English Lyrics
Old Bohemian Melody

See the loveliest blooming rose, Hallelujah!
From the branch of Jesse grows, Hallelujah!
Chorus

Into flesh is made the Word, Hallelujah!
'Tis our Refuge, Christ the Lord, Hallelujah!
Chorus

Arr. © 2009 by Mel Bay Publications, Inc. (BMI.). All rights Reserved.

Let Us Go, O Shepherds

Starting note: Open fourth string.

Traditional Columbian Carol

Let us go, O shep - herds,

Come ye, one and all;

You will see the Vir - gin

And her Babe so small!

Now this tiny Baby
Came from yonder sky;
Sing a song to please Him,
Sing a lullaby.

Angels told the shepherds,
"Go to Bethlehem,
Hasten to adore Him,
Jesus, Heaven's gem!"

Arr. © 2009 by Mel Bay Publications, Inc. (BMI.). All rights Reserved.

Love Came Down at Christmas

Starting note: Open third string.

Words by Christina Rossi (1830-1894), 1885
Traditional Irish Melody

Love came down at Christ - mas,

Love, all love___ - ly,___ love di - vine;_____

Love was born at Christ - mas,

Star and an - gles gave the sign

Worship we the Godhead,
Love incarnate, love divine;
Worship we our Jesus,
But wherewith the sacred sign?

Love shall be our token,
Love be yours and love be mine;
Love to God and to all men,
Love for plea and gift and sign.

Arr. © 2009 by Mel Bay Publications, Inc. (BMI.). All rights Reserved.

Mary Had a Baby

Starting note: Open third string.

Traditional Spiritual

What did she name Him, my Lord, (3x)
The people keep a-coming and the train done gone.

Named Him Jesus, my Lord . . .

Where was He born, my Lord . . .

Born in a stable, my Lord . . .

Where did she lay Him, my Lord . . .

Laid Him in a manger, my Lord . . .

Arr. © 2009 by Mel Bay Publications, Inc. (BMI.). All rights Reserved.

O Come, Little Children

Starting note: Second string, third fret.

German Carol

O come, lit - tle chil - dren, from cot and from hall, O
come to the man - ger in Beth - le - hem's stall. There
meek - ly He li - eth, the heav - en - ly Child, So
poor and so hum - ble, so sweet and so mild.

2. He's born in a stable for you and for me,
   Draw near by the bright gleaming starlight to see;
   In swaddling clothes lying meek and so mild,
   And purer than angels the heavenly Child.

3. The hay is His pillow, the manger His bed,
   The beasts stand in wonder to gaze on His head;
   Yet there where He lieth, so weak and so poor,
   Come shepherds and wise men to kneel at His door.

4. Oh see, in the cradle, this night in the stall,
   O see how the light dazzles even us all;
   In pure gleaming white lies this Child, heaven's love,
   More beaut'ous and holy than angels above.

5. See Mary and Joseph, with love beaming eyes,
   Are gazing upon the rude bed where He lies;
   The shepherds are kneeling, with hearts full of love
   While angels sing loud hallelujahs above.

Arr. © 2009 by Mel Bay Publications, Inc. (BMI.). All rights Reserved.

Oh Christmas Tree!

Starting note: Open fourth string.

Traditional German Carol

Arr. © 2009 by Mel Bay Publications, Inc. (BMI.). All rights Reserved.

O Christmas tree, O Christmas tree!
You fill our hearts with gladness;
O Christmas tree, O Christmas tree!
You fill our hearts with gladness.
At Christmas time your lovely sight
Fills all our spirits with delight.
O Christmas tree, O Christmas tree!
You fill our hearts with gladness.

O Christmas tree, O Christmas tree!
You are the tree most lovely;
O Christmas tree, O Christmas tree!
You are the tree most lovely.
At Christmas time you bring delight,
Your snowy branches gleam at night.
O Christmas tree, O Christmas tree!
You are the tree most lovely;

Once in Royal David's City

Starting note: Open fourth string.

Lyrics by Cecil F. Alexander, 1848
Music by Henry J. Gauntlett, 1858

Arr. © 2009 by Mel Bay Publications, Inc. (BMI.). All rights Reserved.

He came down to earth from Heaven,
Who is God and Lord of all,
And His shelter was a stable,
And His cradle was a stall;
With the poor, and mean, and lowly,
Lived on earth our Savior holy.

And, through all His wondrous childhood,
He would honor and obey,
Love and watch the lowly maiden,
In whose gentle arms He lay;
Christian children all must be
Mild, obedient, good as He.

For He is our childhood's pattern;
Day by day, like us He grew,
He was little, weak and helpless,
Tears and smiles like us He knew;
And He feeleth for our sadness,
And He shareth in our gladness.

And our eyes at last shall see Him,
Through His own redeeming love,
For that Child so dear and gentle
Is our Lord in Heav'n above;
And He leads His children on
To the place where He is gone.

Not in that poor lowly stable,
With the oxen standing by,
We shall see Him; but in Heaven,
Set at God's right hand on high;
Where like stars His children crowned
All in white shall wait around.

Out of the Orient Crystal Skies

Starting note: Open third string.

Traditional English Carol

Out of the O - rient cry - stal skies A

blaz - ing star did shine _____ Show_____ -

ing the place_____ where poor - ly lies A

bless_____ - ed Babe di - vine._____

2. Born of a maid of royal blood
   Who Mary hight by name;
   A sacred rose which once did bud
   By grace of heavenly flame.

3. This shining star three kings did guide
   Even from the furthest East;
   To Bethlehem where it betide
   This blessed Babe did rest,

4. Laid in a silly manger poor,
   Betwixt an ox and ass;
   Whom these three kings did all adore
   As God's high pleasure was.

5. And for the joy of His great birth
   A thousand angels sing:
   "Glory and peace unto the earth
   Where born is this new King!"

6. The shepherds dwelling thee about,
   Where they this news did know;
   Came singing all even in a rout,
   "Falan-tiding-dido!"

Arr. © 2009 by Mel Bay Publications, Inc. (BMI.). All rights Reserved.

Over the River and Through the Woods

Starting note: Open fourth string.

Lydia Maria Child

Over the river and through the woods,
To have a first-rate play;
Oh hear the bells ring, "Ting-a-ling-ling!"
Hurrah for Thanksgiving Day, hey!
Over the river and through the woods,
Trot fast my dapple gray!
Spring over the ground, like a hunting hound!
For this is Thanksgiving Day, hey!

Arr. © 2009 by Mel Bay Publications, Inc. (BMI.). All rights Reserved.

The Seven Blessings of Mary

Starting note: Second string, third fret.

Traditional Appalachian Carol

Arr. © 2009 by Mel Bay Publications, Inc. (BMI.). All rights Reserved.

The very next Blessing that Mary had,
It was the blessing of two;
To think her little Jesus
Could read the Bible through,
Could read the Bible through.
Chorus

The very next blessing that Mary had,
It was the blessing of three;
To think her little Jesus
Could make the blind to see,
Could make the blind to see.
Chorus

The very next blessing that Mary had,
It was the blessing of four;
To think her little Jesus
Could make the rich to poor,
Could make the rich to poor.
Chorus

The very next blessing that Mary had,
It was the blessing of five;
To think her little Jesus
Could make the dead to rise,
Could make the dead to rise.
Chorus

The very next blessing that Mary had,
It was the blessing of six;
To think her little Jesus
Could make the well to sick,
Could make the well to sick.
Chorus

The very next blessing that Mary had,
It was the blessing of seven;
To think her little Jesus
Had gone away to heaven,
Had gone away to heaven.
Chorus

Shepherds, Shake off Your Drowsy Sleep

Starting note: Open third string.

Traditional French Carol

Shep - herds! shake off your drow - sy sleep, Rise and leave your sil - ly_____ sheep; An - gels from heav'n a - round loud sing - ing, Tid_____ - ings of_____ great joy_____ are bring - ing. Shep - herds! the cho - rus come and swell! Sing No - el, oh sing_____ No - el.

Arr. © 2009 by Mel Bay Publications, Inc. (BMI.). All rights Reserved.

Hark! Even now the bells ring 'round,
Listen to their merry sound;
Hark! How the birds new songs are making,
As if winter's chains were breaking.
Chorus

See how the flowers all burst anew,
Thinking snow is summer dew;
See how the stars afresh are glowing,
All their brightest beams bestowing.
Chorus

Cometh at length the age of peace,
Strife and sorrow now shall cease;
Prophets foretold the wondrous story
Of this Heaven-born Prince of Glory.
Chorus

Shepherds! Then up and quick away,
Seek the Babe ere break of day;
He is the hope of every nation,
All in Him shall find salvation.
Chorus

Silent Night

Starting note: Open fourth string.

Words by Joseph Mohr
Music by Franz Gruber

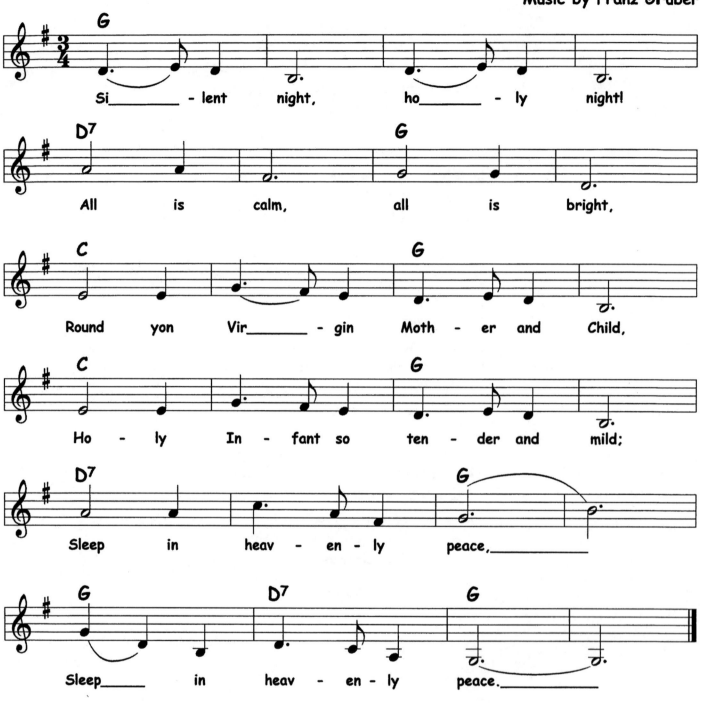

Si - lent night, ho - ly night!

All is calm, all is bright,

Round yon Vir - gin Moth - er and Child,

Ho - ly In - fant so ten - der and mild;

Sleep in heav - en - ly peace,

Sleep in heav - en - ly peace.

Silent Night, holy night,
Shepherds quake at the sight,
Glories stream from heaven afar,
Heavenly hosts sing Alleluia;
Christ the Savior is born!
Christ the Savior is born!

Silent Night, holy night,
Son of God love's pure light,
Radiant beams from Thy holy face,
With the dawn of redeeming grace;
Jesus, Lord, at Thy birth,
Jesus, Lord at Thy birth.

Arr. © 2009 by Mel Bay Publications, Inc. (BMI.). All rights Reserved.

The Sussex Carol
(On Christmas Night, All Christians Sing)

Starting note: Second string, third fret.

Traditional English Carol

Then why should men on earth be sad, since our Redeemer made us glad,
Then why should men on earth be sad, since our Redeemer made us glad;
When from our sin He set us free, all for to gain our liberty.

Arr. © 2009 by Mel Bay Publications, Inc. (BMI.). All rights Reserved.

Up on the Housetop

Starting note: Second string, third fret.

Benjamin R. Hanby, 1866

Arr. © 2009 by Mel Bay Publications, Inc. (BMI.). All rights Reserved.

First comes the stocking of little Nell,
Oh, dear Santa, fill it well;
Give her a dolly that laughs and cries,
One that will open and shut her eyes.
Chorus

Next comes the stocking of little Will,
Oh, just see what a glorious fill;
Here is a hammer and lots of tacks,
Also a ball and a whip that cracks.
Chorus

The Virgin Mary Had a Baby Boy

Starting note: Open fourth string.

Traditional West Indian Melody

Arr. © 2009 by Mel Bay Publications, Inc. (BMI.). All rights Reserved.

The angels sang when the baby was born,
The angels sang when the baby was born,
The angels sang when the baby was born,
And proclaimed Him the Savior Jesus.
Chorus

The wise men saw where the baby was born,
The wise men saw where the baby was born,
The wise men saw where the baby was born,
And they saw that His name was Jesus.
Chorus

We Wish You a Merry Christmas

Starting note: Open fourth string.

Traditional English Carol

Arr. © 2009 by Mel Bay Publications, Inc. (BMI.). All rights Reserved.

Oh, bring us a figgy pudding,
Oh, bring us a figgy pudding;
Oh, bring us a figgy pudding
And a cup of good cheer.
Refrain

We won't go until we get some,
We won't go until we get some;
We won't go until we get some,
So bring some out here.
Refrain

We all love our figgy pudding,
We all love our figgy pudding;
We all love our figgy pudding
With a cup of good cheer.
Refrain

We wish you a Merry Christmas,
We wish you a Merry Christmas;
We wish you a Merry Christmas
And a Happy New Year.
Refrain

To wish you A Merry Christmas

While Shepherds Watched Their Flocks by Night

Starting note: Second string, third fret.

Old English Melody
Lyrics by Nahum Tate (1652-1715)

Arr. © 2009 by Mel Bay Publications, Inc. (BMI.). All rights Reserved.

"To you in David's town this day
Is born of David's line,
The Savior who is Christ, the Lord
And this shall be the sign:
The heav'nly Babe you there shall find
To human-view displayed,
All meanly wrapped in swathing bands
And in a manger laid."

Thus spake the seraph, and forthwith
Appeared a shining throng
Of angels, praising God, who thus
Addressed their joyful song:
"All glory be to God on high
And to the earth be peace;
Good will henceforth from heav'n to men
Begin and never cease."

Do you enjoy this music book?

**Mel Bay Publications offers an exciting variety
of 3-chord songbooks by Larry McCabe:**

101 Three-Chord Songs for Guitar, Banjo, and Uke (MB99476)

101 Three-Chord Children's Songs for Guitar, Banjo, and Uke (MB21279)

101 Three-Chord Hymns and Gospel Songs for Guitar, Banjo, and Uke (MB21280)

101 Three-Chord Country and Bluegrass Songs for Guitar, Banjo, and Uke (MB21282)

50 Three-Chord Christmas Songs for Guitar, Banjo, and Uke (MB21281)